THE BIRDMAKER'S NEST

A StoryPenned By Erika & Robb Brunson
Illustrated by Erika Brunson

This book is dedicated to our friends and family,
every person who made a hospital visit,
and every person who made us dinner.

For every note written,
grace given, and
prayer uttered,
we are grateful.

Today is special. This is the very first watercolor I painted. Grief is over-whelming to say the least. God allowed me to paint my way through my grief, and in doing so, left me wide open to His sneaky, steadfast, faithful love. Art isn't the therapy… …Jesus is. all the time spent paint-ing He stayed. He didn't just stay…He participated. He bound up my broken heart with His very own self, while did the only thing I could do… …paint. This picture is special because I call Robb, 'Bear' and the little birdies on his back are our kids. If you re going through a terrible time, it's nice to ave a Robb, but crucial to have Jesus.

THE BIRDMAKER'S NEST is our expression of grief. My husband Robb and I have lost 4 children; two of them to stillbirth. Their names are Millicent Hope and Judah Ellis. We call them Millie and Judah. Creating the artwork and words in this book are two of the ways I began to grieve them. When Millie died we threw her a party. I overheard Robb say to someone in attendance, "When we're sad we craft." It's true. We just had to create. Weeping, screaming, and throwing things was also a part of the process, but that's the part you would expect. What I didn't expect was for God to make me a creator of pictures as I was denied being a creator of people.

Still, we have no living children, but we do have a very good God who meets the deepest longing in us with His very own presence. We are full of joy and blessed, and no doubt still longing for children.

Often we have found ourselves wanting to reflect on the truth and beauty of Millie and Judah's lives. We wanted to have a place to honor them, and to have something beautiful to hold when reflecting on their little lives. For this very reason we thought this bo might be helpful for you as well. The page to the right is for your child or children's names and any other details you'd like to mention about your sweet babies.

More than anything else Robb and I would like you to know that you are not alone.

"Look! An egg is in our nest," a cozy birdie case. Momma snuggled up tightly to keep her baby safe.

Without any warning their baby bird broke free. She flapped her wings, fluttered in the air, and too quickly left their tree.

Daddy bird and Momma named their little birdie Millie. "She's one of us, so we know she will be silly - and beautiful,

and talented,

and loved,

and adored.

How can we live without seeing our Millie-bird soar?"

"Our Millie-bird has left us,"
Momma and Daddy sadly cried.

Hearing their mourning the
Birdmaker flew to their side.
He made them a promise,
and it was indeed the best
"Your Millie-bird is happy,
whole, and resting in My Nest."

"It makes us so sad to have had a short time with her.

We love her so much, let's hatch another bird."

Judah was loved
as much as his sister.
Unfortunatly, he was here
and gone even quicker.

Before the changing of the leaves
it cracked their hearts to see,
their birdie boy flying up
to the Birdmaker's tree.

Sweet Momma bird ached
perched in her empty nest.

"Where are you my little birds?
Why fly away so fast?"

When Millie-bird flew,
Momma screeched like an owl
with Judah not a peep, not a sound.

If she'd leapt to persue,
the weight of losing the two
would have pulled her
                         to the ground.

She knew they were a gift from
the One who makes the birds,
but she could not understand
why He kept collecting hers.

Daddy bird landed and
quietly nestled in.
He and Momma chirped sadly,
"We have an empty nest again.

What if another birdie
falls from it's nest?
Perhaps it would enjoy
living in our tree best."

Just before the door
of their birdie hearts shut
the thought of a bird alone
opened them back up.

"Wherever you are, little birdie,
will you be ours?
Like our love for Millie and Judah
our love for you grows every hour

No matter where you are
the Birdmaker sees you.
He sees you, and loves you...
...and He loves us, too.

As we sit in our nest
mourning our two,
our sad tears mix
with glad tears
at the possibility of you."

For our sweet Millie,
our beautiful boy Judah,
and the one we wait for...
We love all our tender chicks.

From grief to grief searching
for the one He has for us -

The trail we blaze
with the Birdmaker
is an adventure, and
He is more than enough.

Love
Momma & Da

Erika & Robb 10/2007